# FUN WITH
# SIMPLE SCIENCE

# Floating and Sinking

KINGFISHER BOOKS

# FLOATING AND SINKING

In this book, you can discover what makes things float or sink and find out how to design the fastest boat.
The book is divided into seven different topics. Look out for the big headings with a circle at each end – like the one at the top of this page. These headings tell you where a new topic starts.

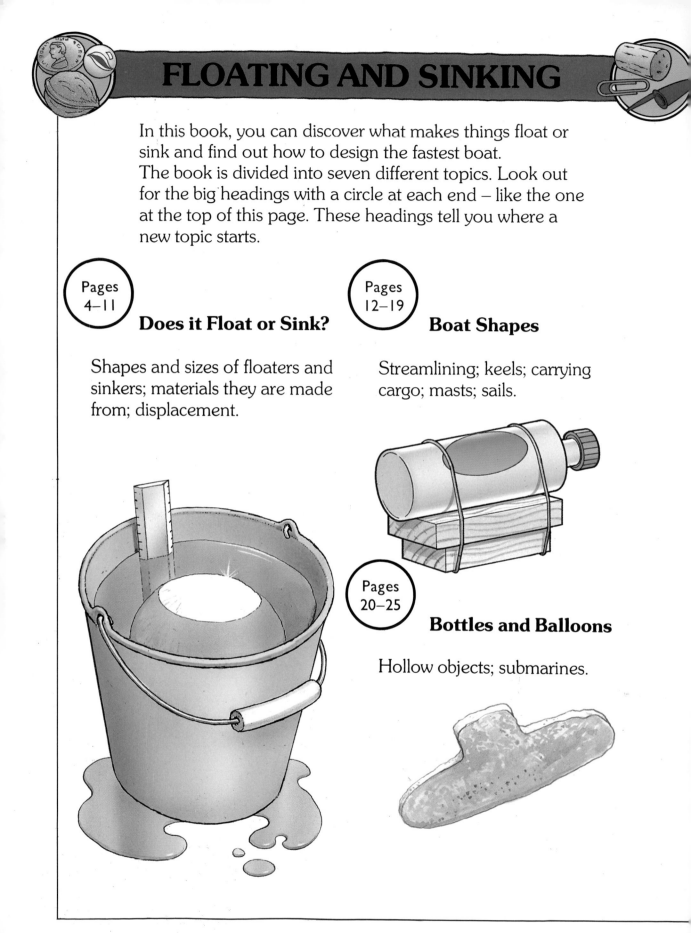

Pages 4–11

### Does it Float or Sink?

Shapes and sizes of floaters and sinkers; materials they are made from; displacement.

Pages 12–19

### Boat Shapes

Streamlining; keels; carrying cargo; masts; sails.

Pages 20–25

### Bottles and Balloons

Hollow objects; submarines.

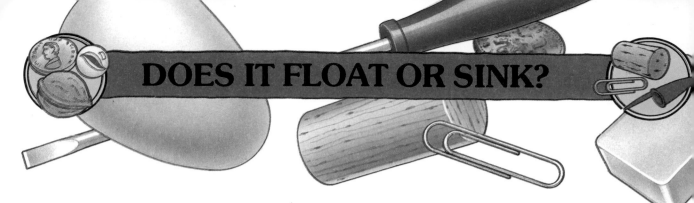

Look at the objects along the edges of these two pages.
Which objects will float in water? Which will sink?

Make your own collection of objects to test. Choose
things that are different shapes, sizes and weights. Try to
find things made from different materials, such as paper,
wood or plastic.

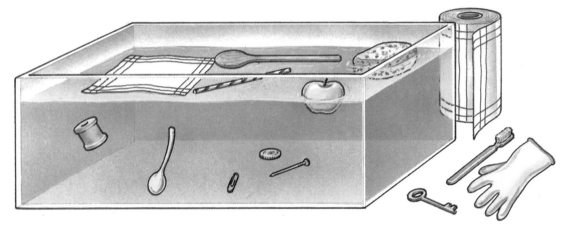

Fill a large bowl, a tank or the bath with water. Put your
collection of objects into the water one at a time. Before
you put each object into the water, see if you can guess
whether it will float or sink.

▶ Next time you are at the seaside or near a lake or a river,
look carefully at any boats floating on the water. Which
materials are they made from? What shape are they? You can
find out more about boats on pages 12–19.

## Floaters and Sinkers

To keep a record of the floaters and sinkers you discover, you could draw a chart like this one.

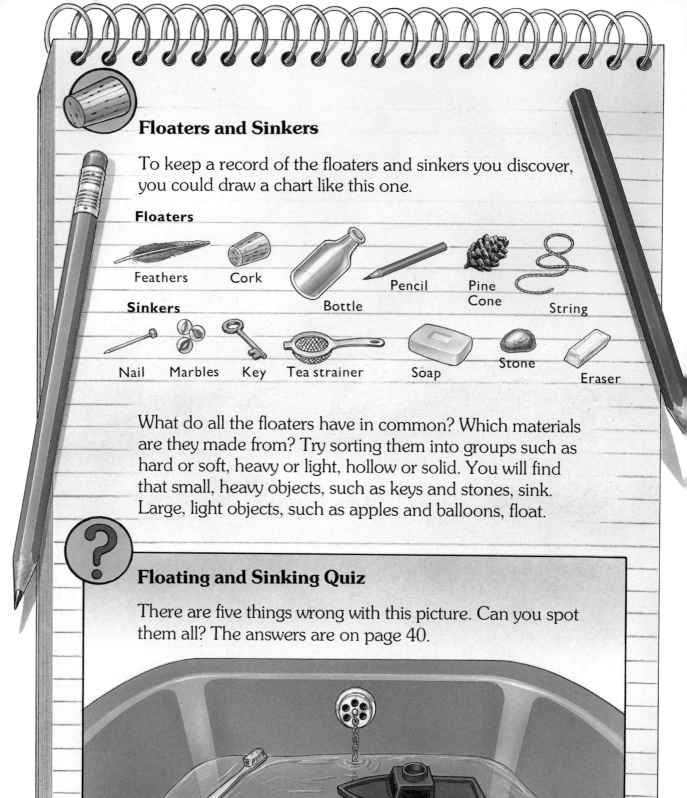

### Floaters

Feathers  Cork  Bottle  Pencil  Pine Cone  String

### Sinkers

Nail  Marbles  Key  Tea strainer  Soap  Stone  Eraser

What do all the floaters have in common? Which materials are they made from? Try sorting them into groups such as hard or soft, heavy or light, hollow or solid. You will find that small, heavy objects, such as keys and stones, sink. Large, light objects, such as apples and balloons, float.

### Floating and Sinking Quiz

There are five things wrong with this picture. Can you spot them all? The answers are on page 40.

## Making Floaters Sink

Did you find any objects that sometimes float and sometimes sink? For example, a paper towel floats at first but it soon soaks up the water and sinks. A limpet shell floats one way up but if you turn it over, it sinks. This photograph shows a submersible. When parts of it are filled with water, it sinks below the surface.

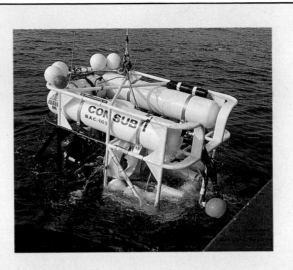

Sponge

The air holes in a sponge make it float high out of the water. Squeeze the sponge under the water. Can you see bubbles of air coming out of the sponge? When you let go of the squeezed sponge, how high does it float?

Tiny holes in the peel of a lemon contain air bubbles. The air makes the lemon float in water. But if you peel a lemon, it sinks! Try peeling an apple. Does this make the apple sink?

Turn to page 20 to find out more about things filled with air.

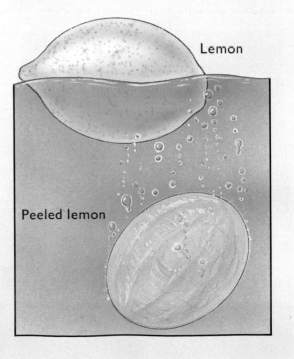

Lemon

Peeled lemon

## Floaters

Sort your floaters into groups according to the materials they are made from. You should use groups such as wood, plastics, rubber, fabrics (wool, cotton, string and so on).

### Does all Wood Float?

Collect some different types of wood, such as oak, balsa wood, mahogany, pine, deal and ebony. A timber merchant may let you have small pieces. Put the wood into a bowl of water. Use blocks of wood which are about the same size.

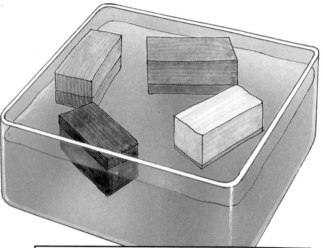

▼ In some countries, tree trunks from the forest float down a river to reach the saw mill.

### What happens
You will find that the different types of wood float at different levels in the water. Balsa wood is very light and floats high out of the water. Ebony is so heavy, it sinks.

## Icebergs

Huge lumps of ice floating in the sea are called icebergs. Only about a tenth of an iceberg shows above the surface of the water. This makes icebergs very dangerous to ships.

## Make an Iceberg

### You will need:
a balloon, water, a freezer, a ruler, scissors.

1. Fit the balloon over a cold tap and fill it with water.
2. Ask an adult to help you tie the end of the balloon to seal the water inside.
3. Put the balloon inside a plastic bag (without holes) and leave the bag in a freezer overnight.
4. Next morning, take the balloon out of the freezer and use the scissors to cut away the balloon carefully.
5. Put your iceberg in a deep bucket of water. It will float, but only just. How much ice is below the water?

## Water Pushes Back

Try to push a tennis ball under the water in a bowl. What can you feel? Then let go. What happens?

It's hard to push the ball under the water because the water pushes back. When you let go of the ball, the water pushes it back to the surface again. The upward push of water is called upthrust. An object floats if the upthrust of the water is strong enough to support its weight.

Try the same experiment with a block of polystyrene or a larger ball, such as a soccer ball. Do you have to push harder? What happens when you let go?

## Make a Water Candle

How can a candle stay alight underwater? Try this investigation to find out.

**You will need:**
a night-light candle, matches, a jar of water, a marker pen.

1. Fill the jar with water almost to the top.
2. Float the candle on the water. Make sure the candle and the wick do not get wet.

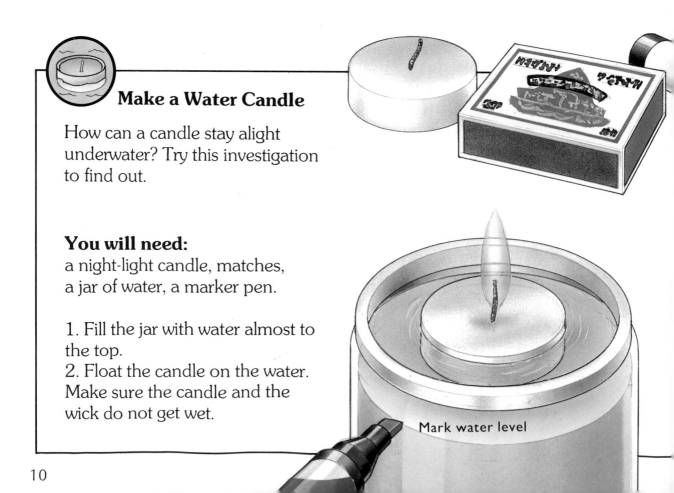

Mark water level

## Pushing Water out of the Way

Next time you get into a bath, watch the level of the water. To make room for itself, your body pushes some of the water out of the way and the level goes up. This is called displacement. You can use displacement to measure the amount of space your thumb takes up (its volume). You will need a plastic bottle and a measuring jug.

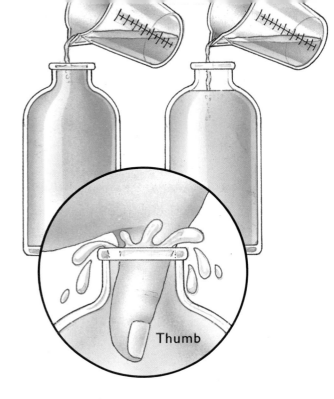

Thumb

1. Fill the bottle with water right up to the top.
2. Stick your thumb into the bottle as far as it will go. Some of the water will spill over the edge.
3. Now use the measuring jug to fill the bottle up to the top again. The amount of water you use to do this is equal to the volume of your thumb.

### What happens

As the candle burns, it gets lighter and floats higher in the water. Because the candle pushes less water up the sides of the jar, the water level goes down.

Wall of wax stops water reaching flame.

3. Use the pen to mark the level of the water on the side of the jar.
4. Ask an adult to help you light the candle. Watch what happens. How long does your water candle last?

# BOAT SHAPES

A ball of modelling clay sinks in water. But if you make the same ball of clay into a boat shape, it floats. The wide, flat boat shape pushes away more water than the narrow, round ball. The water pushes back harder against the flat shape and this holds it up on the surface of the water.

## Find the Fastest Shape

Some boats, such as tugboats, are built to be strong and stable, or difficult to tip over. Other boats, such as power boats, are shaped to help them zoom through the water at high speed. This is called a streamlined shape.

Test some boat shapes yourself. Float your boats in a long piece of plastic guttering with two end pieces.

### Sample shapes

Cut the boats out of thin balsa wood and use the same amount of wood for each boat.

Attach a weight to a long piece of thread and pin the other end of the thread to the front of each boat in turn. Measure the time each boat takes to travel the same distance. Which shape is fastest?

Gutter

Weight

## Staying Upright

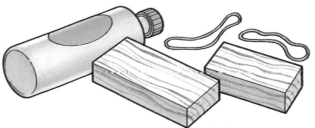

Some boats have an extra piece called a keel on the bottom of the main body (the hull). To find out how a keel works, make one yourself.

**You will need:**

an empty plastic bottle, two blocks of wood (one larger than the other), thick elastic bands.

1. Put the bottle into a bowl of water and try tipping it over. You will find that it rolls over quite easily.
2. Now ask an adult to cut two blocks of wood.
3. Use the elastic bands to fix the blocks of wood under the bottle.
4. Float the bottle on the water and try tipping it over again. What happens this time?

## What happens

The keel keeps the weight in the centre of the boat and helps it to balance in a level position on the water. It's hard to make the boat tip right over, or capsize.

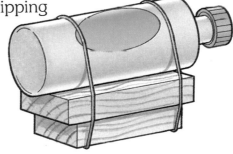

▼ Keels come in all shapes and sizes. A boat with a keel cannot easily sail in shallow water.

## Make a Catamaran

A catamaran is a boat with two hulls. It is a very stable design which will not tip over easily. It does not need a keel to help it stay upright. But if a catamaran does capsize, it's hard to turn it the right way up again.

**You will need:** A washing-up liquid bottle, a small hacksaw, thin strips of balsa wood, waterproof tape, scissors.

1. Ask an adult to cut the washing-up liquid bottle in half with the hacksaw.
2. Use the scissors to cut three narrow strips of balsa wood.
3. Use the tape to stick the balsa wood across the half bottles to match the picture.
4. Try floating your catamaran in water. Can you make it capsize?

## Make Metal Ships

### You will need:

Tin foil, a block of wood, plastic containers, scissors, sticky tape or glue.

1. Cut a piece of foil larger than the block of wood.

2. Fold it around the wood so the sides stand up. How high do the sides have to be to stop the water getting in? Fix the corners with tape or glue.

4. Line the bottom of your metal boat with more foil.

5. Wrap foil around the plastic containers in the same way.

6. Make some more boats using paper instead of foil. Which boats last longer?

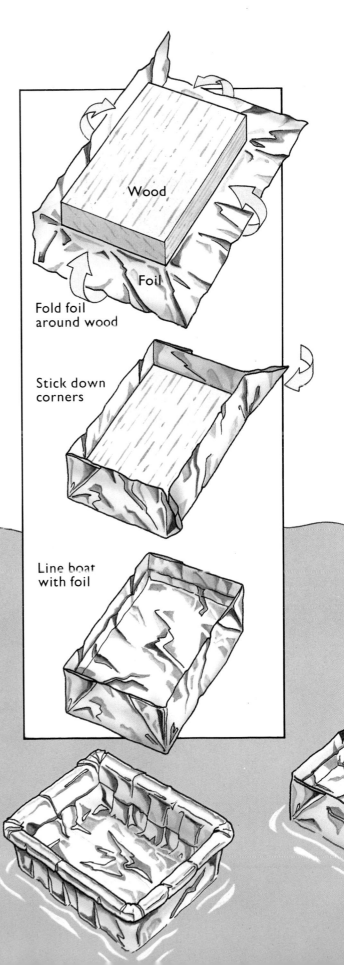

Fold foil around wood

Stick down corners

Line boat with foil

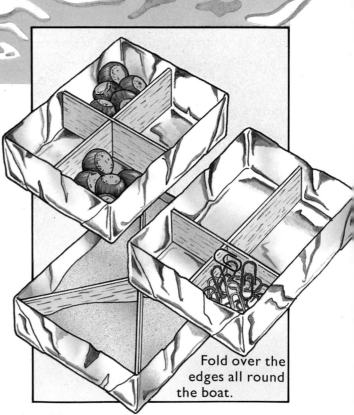

 **How Much Cargo?**

Many boats are made to carry food, cars, books and other kinds of cargo from one place to another. Make some boats out of tin foil and see how much cargo they will carry before they sink. Try boats of different sizes.

Use pieces of thin balsa wood to divide your boats into sections. Load the two end sections with cargo. Or the middle section and one end section. How does this affect the position of the boat?

Fold over the edges all round the boat.

▶ The hold of a container ship is divided into separate sections. This helps to stop the containers moving about as the ship rolls about in rough seas.

## Messing about with Masts

What is the best size and position for the mast on a sailing ship? To find out, cut up some plastic straws to make long, medium length and short masts. Fix each mast in turn onto a balsa wood boat and try tilting the boat to one side. When you let go, does the boat tip over and capsize? Or does it swing back upright again? Put the masts in different positions on the boat.

Mast positions

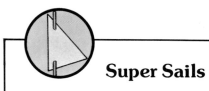

## Super Sails

Make some sails to see how they help a boat to go faster. For the mast, use a straw, a cocktail stick or a piece of thin dowel.

You could make your sails out of paper, cloth or plastic. Blow on each sail or use a paper fan to see which sail makes the boat move fastest. What happens if you blow through a straw on just one side of a sail?

Try different shapes, sizes and numbers of sails.

Push a cocktail stick into the balsa wood and slide the straw mast on top.

## What happens

You should find that the short mast will not make the boat capsize in any position. The medium length mast will make the boat lean over in some positions. The long mast will make the boat capsize in some positons. Where is the best position for a long mast?

▼ How many different kinds of sail can you see on this sailing ship?

# BOTTLES AND BALLOONS

Put some hollow objects into a tank or bath of water.
Try some of these: a plastic mug, a plastic bottle, a bowl, a saucepan, an empty drinks can.

You will find that they all float. Can you make any of them sink?

Try pushing them under the water. Look at all the bubbles of air rising to the surface. Even though hollow things look empty, they are really full of air.

Fill a plastic bottle half full of water and put on the top. The bottle still floats in water. How much water do you have to put inside the bottle before it sinks?

Now try putting some sand inside the bottle instead of water. How much sand do you need to make the bottle sink?

## Lifting Buried Treasure

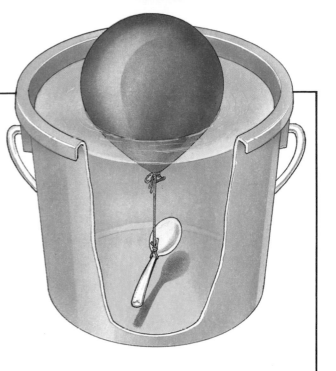

Balloons are full of air so they float high out of the water. If you tie a balloon to a sinker, such as a metal spoon, it will float underneath the balloon. Try different sinkers such as stones, a brick, a mirror, scissors and a screwdriver. Will the balloon lift all these sinkers off the bottom?

▼ Archaeologists use special balloons to lift objects they find on an underwater dig up to the surface.

To find out how submarines dive under the water and rise to the surface again, try these tests.

### Rising Raisins

Put some raisins in the bottom of a clear plastic beaker. Fill the beaker half full of a clear, fizzy drink, such as lemonade. Watch what happens.

The raisins will soon zoom up and down the beaker as if by magic. But it's really science, not magic. Can you work out what makes the raisins move? Look at all the bubbles of air that stick to the raisins. How long do the raisins keep rising?

## Yellow Submarine

### You will need:

a clear jar, a fresh lemon, a
balloon, scissors, an elastic band.

1. Use the scissors to cut a piece
of lemon peel in the shape of a
submarine. Ask an adult for help.
2. Fill the jar with water and put
the lemon peel into the water.
3. Cut a circle from the balloon
and stretch the balloon over the
top of the jar. Hold the balloon in
place with the elastic band.

4. When you press hard on the
balloon with your finger, you will
see your yellow submarine sink
down slightly.
5. When you take your finger off
the balloon, the submarine will
rise up again.

### What happens

Air can be easily compressed into
a smaller space, but water cannot.
As you press on the balloon, you
squash the tiny bubbles of air in
the lemon peel into a smaller
space and let extra water in. This
makes the submarine heavier, so
it sinks a little . When you take
your finger away, the air expands
again, pushing out the water. This
makes the submarine lighter and
it rises up again.

▲ Scientists such as archaeologists, biologists or engineers may use small submarines to help them examine shipwrecks, living things or man-made structures under the sea.

## Bottle Submarine

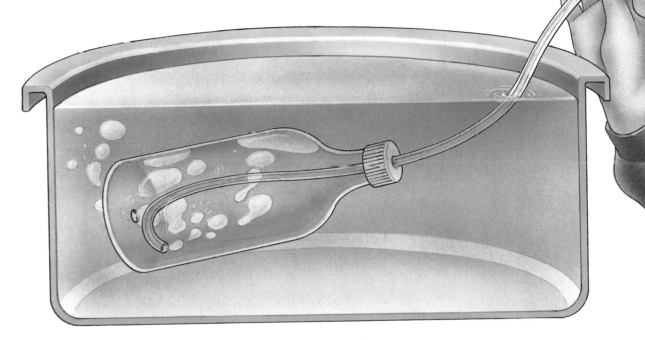

Submarines dive by filling tanks inside the submarine with water. They rise by pumping water out of the tanks again. If the tanks contain a lot of air, the submarine becomes lighter and rises. Make your own submarine to see how this works.

### You will need:

a plastic bottle with a lid, a bowl of water, a short length of plastic tubing.

1. Ask an adult to help you make a hole in the lid of the bottle and another hole in the bottom of the bottle.
2. Ask a friend to hold their finger over the hole in the bottom of the bottle and fill it with as much water as you can.

3. Push the tubing through the hole in the bottle top and put the top on the bottle.
4. Lower the bottle carefully into the bowl of water and blow hard down the plastic tube.

### What happens

As the air from your lungs goes inside the bottle, it pushes out some of the water. So the bottle rises, just like a real submarine.

25

# WATER'S STRETCHY SKIN

Watch water dripping from a tap. There is a special force on the surface of water which pulls it inwards. This force is called surface tension. It gives water drops their smooth, round shape. It also makes water look as if it has a stretchy 'skin' on the surface.

### Crazy Colours

Soap or washing-up liquid breaks down the surface tension of water and stops the skin forming. This stops water sticking together in drops and so it flows more easily into all the places where dirt collects. This is one reason why water is better at cleaning things when we add soap or washing-up liquid.

To see what happens when water loses its skin, try this test.

Fill a shallow dish or saucer with milk and put a few drops of food colouring on top of the milk. Use a spoon to drop a small amount of washing-up liquid on top of the colour and watch the colours explode. How long does the swirling movement last? Can you think why it stops?

Food colouring

## Spinning Snowman

**You will need:**

a bowl of water, a cork, thin balsa wood, four cocktail sticks, moth balls, paper, scissors, glue or sticky tape, crayons.

1. Draw and colour a small snowman on the paper and cut it out.
2. Ask an adult to help you cut a slice off the cork. Cut out four small pieces of balsa wood.
3. Stick the snowman to the slice of cork.
4. Make a small notch in each of the small pieces of balsa wood and wedge a piece of moth ball into each notch.
5. Stick the four cocktail sticks into the slice of cork to make a cross shape.
6. Fix the small pieces of balsa wood at the ends of the cocktail sticks.
7. Put your snowman into the bowl of water and watch it spin around.

### What happens

The moth balls weaken the pull of the surface tension in the water close to them. The stronger pull of the tension in front of each moth ball pulls the sticks and the snowman around in a circle. How long does the snowman keep spinning?

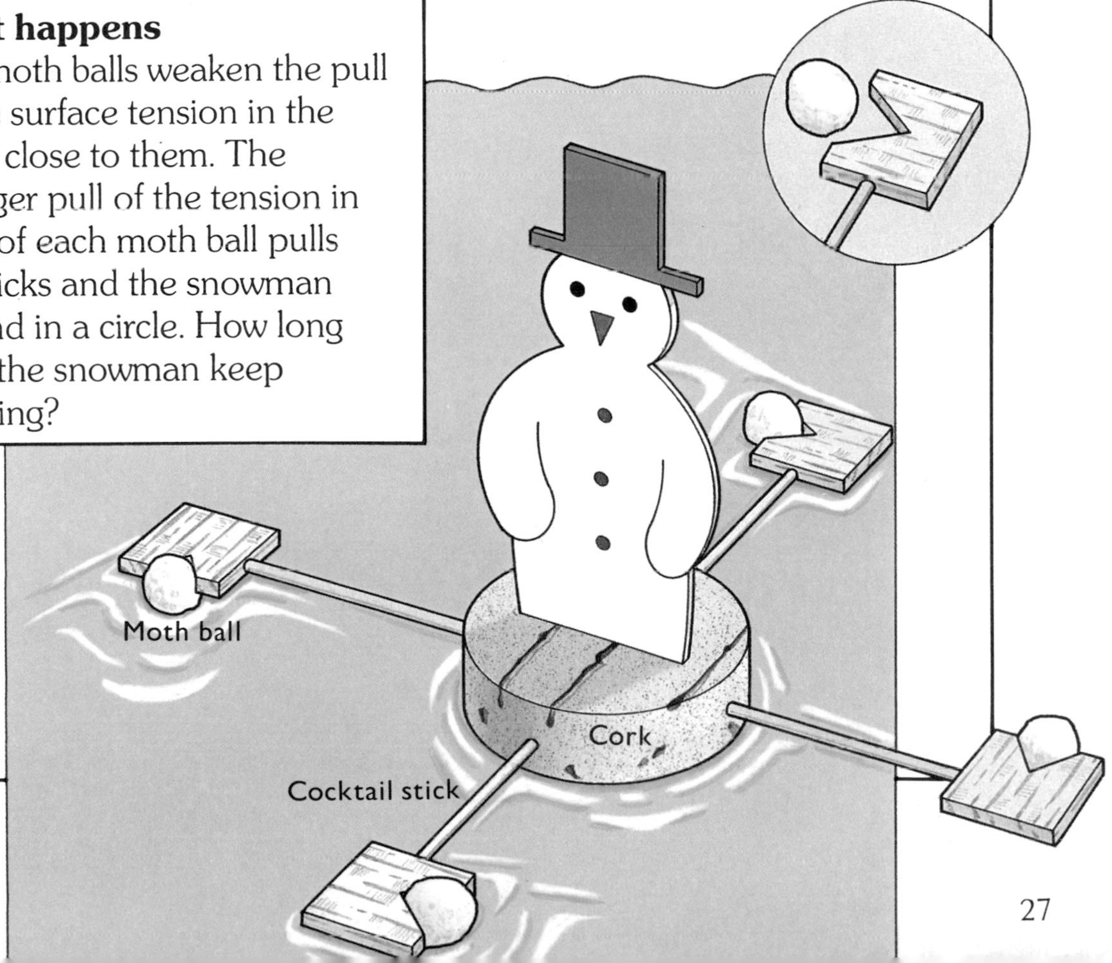

Moth ball

Cork

Cocktail stick

# FLOATING LIQUIDS

To measure how things float in different liquids, scientists use an instrument called a hydrometer. The hydrometer sinks farther into some liquids than others. To see how it works, make one yourself.

## Make a hydrometer

Cut about six centimetres off a straw and push a small blob of modelling clay on to the end. Use a thick pencil to mark a line on the straw every five millimetres.

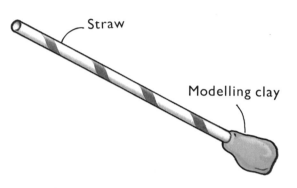

Straw

Modelling clay

Try floating your hydrometer in ordinary water, salty water and surgical spirit. How does it float each time?

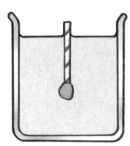

Surgical spirit

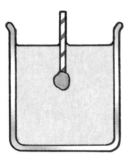

Tap water

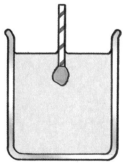

Salt water

## What happens

Salty water is heavier than ordinary water so it pushes harder against objects floating in it. To float in salty water, objects need to displace less water than they do in ordinary water. So the hydrometer floats higher in salty water. In surgical spirit, the hydrometer floats at a lower level compared to ordinary water. This shows that surgical spirit is lighter than water.

## Salty Surprises

An egg usually sinks in water but this trick shows you how to make an egg look as if it floats in water. First you need to make some very salty water.

1. Pour some warm water into a saucepan and add some salt.
2. Stir with a spoon and keep adding salt until you feel a gritty layer building up on the bottom of the pan.
3. Leave the salty water for several hours until it is no longer cloudy. Then it is ready to use.
4. Half fill a large jar with the salty water and put the egg into the water.
5. Now carefully pour some ordinary tap water down the side of the jar. What happens?

Fresh water

Egg

Salt water

### What happens

The tap water is lighter than the salty water so it floats on top. The egg sinks down through the tap water but floats on top of the salty water. It looks as if it is floating in the middle of the jar.

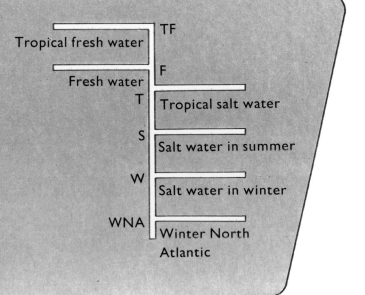

## The Plimsoll Line

A ship floats at different levels depending on the weight of the cargo, the temperature of the water and how much salt is in the water. It floats lower in fresh water than in salt water. And it floats lower in warm water than in cold water. The mark called the Plimsoll line shows the safe level for a fully loaded ship in different types of water.

TF
Tropical fresh water

F
Fresh water

T
Tropical salt water

S
Salt water in summer

W
Salt water in winter

WNA
Winter North Atlantic

## Rainbow Sandwich

To find out more about how liquids float, make a rainbow sandwich.

Add food colour.

Pour oil down the side of the bottle.

Surgical spirit and food colour

Cooking oil

Water and food colour

**You will need:**
a tall, thin bottle (such as a test tube, a medicine or perfume bottle or an olive jar), cooking oil, surgical spirit, two different food colours.

1. Fill the bottle about a third full of water and add a few drops of one food colour.
2. Carefully pour oil down the side of the bottle. It will float because oil is lighter than water.
3. Now add a layer of surgical spirit. This is lighter than oil, so it floats on top of the oil. To colour the top of your sandwich, add a few drops of a different food colour.
4. If your bottle has a lid, you can try turning your sandwich upside down. Be careful to keep the surgical spirit and water apart. If they touch each other, they will mix together and you will lose half your sandwich. If this happens, start again.

▶ Workers try to collect oil which floated on top of the sea water until tides and currents washed it on to the beach.

## Make a Salad Dressing

Do you know why you have to shake salad dressing before you pour it on a salad? Make some yourself to find out.

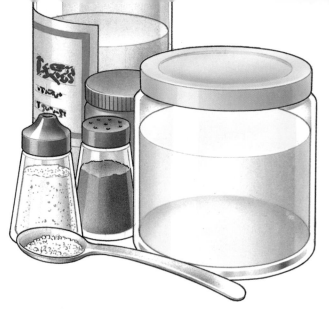

### You will need:

1 tablespoon vinegar, 2 tablespoons salad oil, $\frac{1}{4}$ level teaspoon salt, some pepper, $\frac{1}{4}$ level teaspoon dry mustard, $\frac{1}{4}$ level teaspoon sugar.

1. Put the salt, pepper, mustard and sugar into a bowl.
2. Pour on the vinegar and stir with a spoon to mix everything together.
3. Add the oil a little at a time. Each time you add more oil, beat the mixture with a fork.
4. Put the salad dressing in a bottle in the fridge.

5. After a while, the dressing will settle into layers. What is the top layer made of?
6. Make sure the lid is tightly on the bottle and shake it hard. What happens to the layers?

### What happens

Vinegar contains water, which won't mix with the oil. The oil is lighter than the vinegar so it floats to the top of the bottle and stays there. When you shake the dressing, the oil breaks up into little drops which hang in the vinegar for a while. This makes the dressing look cloudy. How long does the dressing take to go back into layers? If you shake the dressing for longer, can you see any difference in the size of the oil drops?

## The Floating Circle

This trick with floating liquids will help you understand more about why things float.

Coloured water

Add oil

Add surgical spirit

### You will need:

surgical spirit, cooking oil, green food colouring, water, a funnel, a small, flat bottle.

1. Fill the bottle about half full of water.
2. Add a few drops of green food colouring.
3. Use the funnel to pour a few spoonfuls of oil into the bottle.
4. Now add some surgical spirit and watch how the oily layer bends in the middle.
5. Keep adding the surgical spirit until the oily layer becomes a circle floating in the middle of the green liquids.

After adding surgical spirit

### What happens

When you add the surgical spirit, it mixes with the water and makes the water lighter (less dense). The watery mix pushes up less strongly against the oily layer so the oil starts to sink down into the watery mix. As you add more surgical spirit, the watery mix starts to push on the oil equally from all directions. This makes the oil into the shape of a ball.

## Marbling

By floating oily paints or inks on the surface of water, you can make wonderful swirly patterns to decorate paper. This is called marbling because the patterns are like the ones you can see in pieces of polished marble.

### You will need:

an old bowl, marbling inks or oil paints, plain paper, a straw or old fork, newspaper. (If you don't have any oil paints, use some powder paint mixed with cooking oil.)

Fork

Straws

Inks

Cooking oil

Water

Powder paint

Newspaper

Paper

1. Put plenty of newspaper on the floor and put on an apron.
2. Put the bowl in the middle of the newspaper and fill it half full of water.
3. Drop two or three different colours on to the water in turn. You don't need much of each colour.
4. Use the straw or the fork to swirl the paint carefully around until you make a pattern that you like.
5. Now gently lay a piece of thick paper flat on the surface of the water and quickly lift it off again.
6. Hold the paper over the bowl until most of the water has dripped off into the bowl.
7. Leave the paper to dry.
8. When the paper is dry, you can use it to wrap presents, or cover books or pencils.

**Hint:** To clear the water of old colours, put a paper towel on the surface of the water. It will soak up the colours so you can lift them out of the water.

# SINKING TO THE BOTTOM

Rocks such as sandstone are made of layers of small pieces (or particles) of sand. These settle one on top of the other. This often happens underwater when sandy particles washed off the land by rivers sink down to the bottom of an ocean or lake. As more and more sand collects, the weight presses the layers together and squeezes the water out. Over millions of years, the sand becomes hard enough to form rocks.

You can experiment with soil particles to find out more about how rocks form.

Find a large jar with a lid and put in some garden soil until the jar is about one-third full. Fill the rest of the jar with water. Put on the lid, shake the jar and leave it to settle. After a few days, you should be able to see different layers in the jar.

Each layer is made up of particles of a different size. Are the biggest particles on the top or the bottom?

## Cleaning Water

The way small particles sink down through water is used to help us clean the water we drink. At the waterworks, the dirty water from rivers and wells goes through big tanks where all the 'bits' sink to the bottom and are taken out. Then the water goes through filters made of sand and gravel. These trap other dirt which sinks down through the water and into the sand.

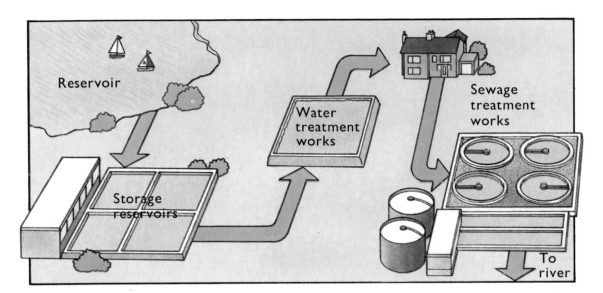

These are filter beds where the dirt is trapped.

Water wings full of air help us to float.

Marlin can reach speeds of up to 80 kilometres per hour. Their streamlined shape helps them to move quickly through the water.

Marlin

Divers wear a weight belt so they can rise and sink.

The sperm whale can dive up to about 3000 metres to search for food. But it has to come to the surface to breathe air after an hour or so.

This seaweed has air bladders to help it to float.

Sperm whale

Bladderwrack

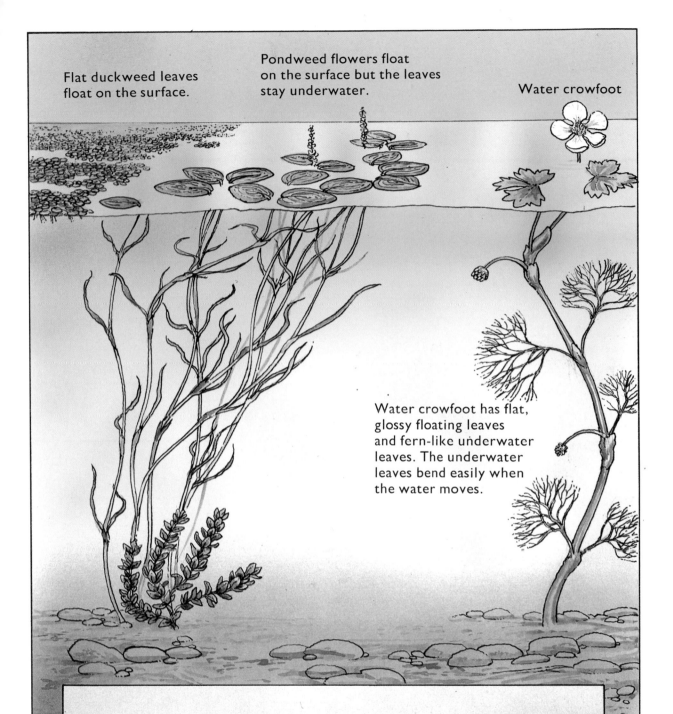

Flat duckweed leaves float on the surface.

Pondweed flowers float on the surface but the leaves stay underwater.

Water crowfoot

Water crowfoot has flat, glossy floating leaves and fern-like underwater leaves. The underwater leaves bend easily when the water moves.

## Floating Green Stuff

Plants that float on or in water have special shapes and structures to help them survive. Most water plants have lots of air spaces inside them to keep them upright and floating in the water.

You can make your own underwater garden in a large tank or jar. Buy or take cuttings of plants such as duckweed, water crowfoot, eelgrass, arrowhead, salvinia and Canadian pondweed.

# INDEX

Page numbers in *italics* refer to illustrations or where illustrations and text occur on the same page.

air 7
  expansion and compression 23
apple 8
archaeologists, underwater *21*, 24

ball 10
balloon *21*
boat 4, 5, *12*, *13* (see also ship)
bottle *20*
bubbles 7

cargo *16–17*
catamaran *14*

clay, modelling 12
colours, crazy 26

displacement *11*, 28

egg *29*

fabrics 8
filter bed *37*
floating 4
floaters 6, *20*

hydrometer *28*

iceberg *9*

keel *13*

lemon 7
liquids 28, *30–31*

marbling *34–35*
marlin *38*

mast *18–19*

oil *30–31*, 32, 33

paint *34–35*
paper towel 7
plants *38–39*
plastic 4
Plimsoll Line *29*

raising, rising *22*
reservoir *37*
rock 36

sails *18–19*
salad dressing *32*
seaweed *38*
*ship, metal* 15
  container *17*
sinkers 6, *20*
sinking 4
snowman, spinning *27*

soil *36*
sperm whale *38*
sponge 7
submarine 22, *23*, *24*, 25
submersible 7
surface tension 26, 27
surgical spirit *30*, 33

tree trunk 8

upthrust 10

water 4, 33
  candle *10–11*
  stretchy skin of *26*
water treatment works *37*
wood 4, 8

**Answers to quiz on page 6:**
These things float: duck, pumice stone.
These things sink: toothbrush, soap, comb.

**Adviser:** Robert Pressling
**Designer:** Ben White
**Editors:** Nicola Barber and Annabel Warburg
**Picture Research:** Elaine Willis

The publishers wish to thank the following artists for contributing to this book:
Peter Bull: page headings, p. 37; Peter Dennis (Linda Rogers Associates): pp. 22/23, 30, 34/35, 36, 38/39; Kuo Kang Chen: pp. 4/5, 20/21, 25, 32/33; John Scorey: pp. 12–19, 26–29.

The publishers also wish to thank the following for providing photographs for this book:
21 Courtesy, J. W. Automarine; 5, 31 Picturepoint; 13, 14 Quadrant; 24 Science Photo Library; 37 Thames Water plc; 17, 19 ZEFA.

Kingfisher Books, Grisewood and Dempsey Ltd, Elsley House, 24–30 Great Titchfield Street, London W1P 7AD

First published in 1990 by Kingfisher Books

Copyright © Grisewood and Dempsey Ltd 1990

**British Library Cataloguing in Publication Data**
Taylor, Barbara
  Floating and sinking.
  1. Floating objects
  I. Title  II. Series
  532'.2

ISBN 0-86272-526-7

Phototypeset by Southern Positives and Negatives (SPAN), Lingfield, Surrey
Colour Separations by Scantrans pte Ltd, Singapore and Newsele Litho, Milan
Printed in Spain